Kingfisher Books, Grisewood and Dempsey Ltd,
Elsley House, 24–30 Great Titchfield Street,
London W1P 7AD

First published in 1990 by Kingfisher Books

Text copyright © Melanie and Chris Rice 1990
Illustrations copyright © Grisewood and Dempsey Ltd 1990

All rights reserved. No part of this publication may
be reproduced, stored in a retrieval system or
transmitted by any means, electronic, mechanical,
photocopying or otherwise, without the prior permission
of the publisher.

BRITISH LIBRARY CATALOGUING IN PUBLICATION DATA
Rice, Melanie
Theatre
1. Theatre – For children
I. Title II. Rice, Chris III. Series
792

ISBN 0-86272-516-X

Edited by Nicola Barber
Designed by Robert Wheeler
Illustrations by Sue Barclay (John Martin & Artists
Ltd), Kevin Maddison, Etchell & Ridyard, Stephen Conlin,
John Scorey, Maggie Brand (Maggie Mundy Artists' Agency)
Cover design by Terry Woodley
With thanks to the staff at the Barbican Theatre, London
Phototypeset by Southern Positives and Negatives (SPAN),
Lingfield, Surrey
Printed in Italy

I like Theatre

Melanie & Chris Rice

KINGFISHER BOOKS

Contents

Telling Stories *8*
Theatres *10*
Getting the Show on the Road *13*
Stage Sets *14*
Stage Machinery *16*
Props and Noises Off *18*
Lighting *20*
See Inside a Theatre *22*
Actors *24*
With and Without Words *26*
Costumes *28*
Masks *30*
Make-up *32*
Clowns *34*
Puppet Theatre *36*
Travelling Theatre *40*
Stage your Own Play *42*
Index *44*

Introducing Theatre

'All the world's a stage.' William Shakespeare wrote these words more than 400 years ago in his play, *As You Like It*. Theatre really is all around us. When people fall in love, or have an argument, or make us laugh, they are doing in real life what actors pretend to do on stage.

This book is about theatre everywhere, from earliest times to the present day. You can read about the places where plays are performed, how actors are trained and how they prepare for a performance. You can read about the other people in theatre – the stagehands, set builders, technicians, producers; no play can go ahead without them. Then there are the different kinds of theatre, Kathakali from India, Bunraku from Japan, mime theatre, puppet theatre, travelling theatre and so on.

We also thought you might like to try out some things for yourself so we have included some activity sections to start you off. Perhaps you would like to try putting on a play of your own? There are some tips in the book to help you but the best ideas will be the ones you have yourself. Have fun!

Chris   Melanie

Telling Stories

A scene from the play *Sir Gawan and the Green Knight* at the London Bubble Theatre.

Everyone enjoys stories, listening to them and telling them. Stories can be made more dramatic by acting them out with words, with dance or with music; on television or on the stage. There are all kinds of stories in the theatre . . .

Everyday stories . . .

Theatres

The Greeks built this theatre (*right*) more than 2300 years ago in Epidaurus. The actors performed in an open space called the 'orchestra'. The audience watched from rows of stone seats arranged like an outspread fan. Behind the orchestra was a storeroom for costumes and props.

In Europe, in the Middle Ages or Medieval times, plays were acted out in the streets. The audience looked on as each scene in the story was presented to them on a separate pageant or cart.

Actors in the Japanese Kabuki Theatre often used a special catwalk (*bottom, left*) called the 'flower way' to leave the stage and walk through the audience.

The Globe Theatre in London was where many of Shakespeare's plays were first performed. The audience either sat in roofed galleries, or stood in front of the stage. Above the stage was a canopy painted blue with golden stars and called 'the heavens'. Backstage there was enough space for costumes, props and machinery. The flag let everyone know that a performance was under way.

In later theatres the audience was separated from the actors by a proscenium arch and curtain. Plays became like moving pictures viewed through a frame.

Many of today's theatres have done away with curtains and proscenium arches, bringing the actors into closer touch with the audience again.

Activity

Make your own toy theatre

You will need a soap powder box (E15 size), card, paints, scissors.

1 Take the box and remove one side panel.

2 Cut out a window from the front measuring 26 × 19cm.

3 Turn the box on its side and cut out slots 3 × 22cm at either end.

4 Behind each slot cut a slit, length 27cm, down from the top edge.

5 Draw some scenery on a piece of card 28 × 38cm, then slide the card into the box between the slits.

6 Draw, then cut out, some actors for your play and stick their feet to strips of card.

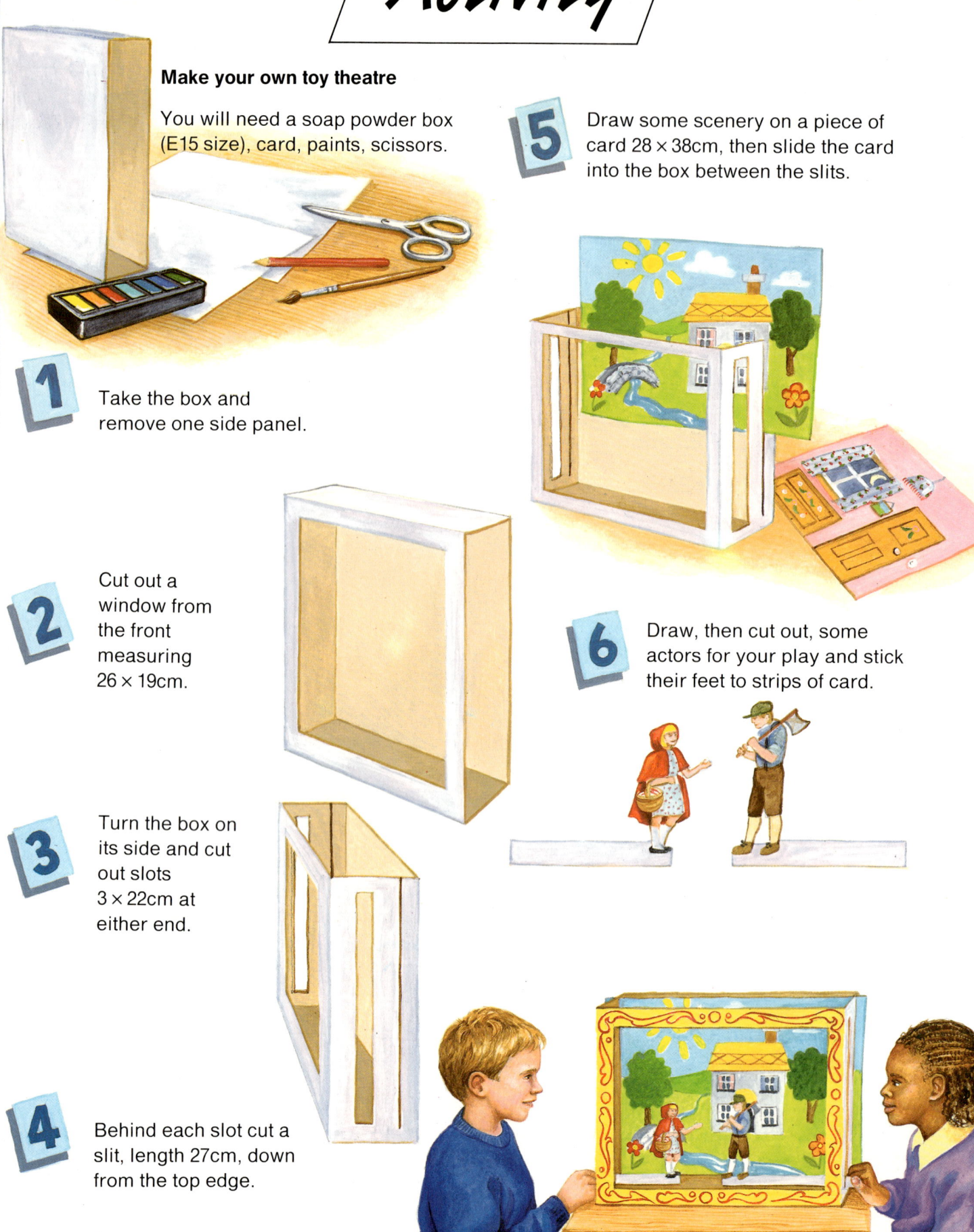

Getting the Show on the Road

The director is often the busiest person in a theatre company, co-ordinating the actors, the designer, the stage manager and the publicity. How many different jobs can you see her doing in the picture below?

1. Planning sets and costumes with the designer.
2. Working behind the scenes with the stage manager and his team.
3. Discussing the script with the author of the play.
4. Leading the actors in rehearsal.
5. Discussing the advertisement of the play with the publicity officer.

Stage Sets

The set helps the audience to imagine what the play is about. It can include a backdrop (painted scene), steps, furniture, walls – anything the designer chooses. Every set is different.

This set was designed by the famous Italian designer, Torelli. He excited his audience by creating a moving sea monster and a flying horse.

The stage set by Giacomo Torelli for Corneille's play *Andromède* (*Andromeda*).

The stage set for Noel Coward's play *Hay Fever*.

Some sets are designed to make a scene look as real as possible . . . others are more fanciful.

The stage set for *The Hostage* designed by Sean Kenny.

14

Backstage

Before the backstage workers begin to build the set, the designer constructs a model of it to show how the scenery is arranged, and to make sure that everything will work.

The skilled workers who construct the set are never seen by the audience, but their work behind the scenes is vital to the performance.

Set painters paint the scenery.

Costumes are made and fitted by the wardrobe mistress.

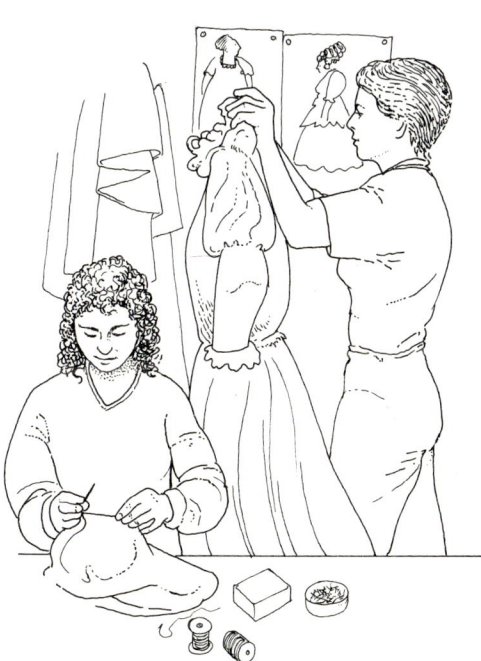

Carpenters build the set and make the props.

The prompt corner

Sometimes actors forget their lines when they are on stage. The prompter gives them cues to help them remember from a prompt corner, hidden from the audience at the side of the stage.

Stage Machinery

Ghosts, gods, demons and fairies... designers sometimes use stage machines to conjure up characters from the spirit world.

Actors can 'fly' across the stage in a flying harness...

descend from the 'heavens' with the help of a winch...

or spring up from the earth through a trap door.

A revolving stage

Quick scene changes can be a problem. Watch this revolving stage turn a kitchen into a garden before your very eyes!

Many plays include fight scenes, but, of course, the weapons used on stage are not real.

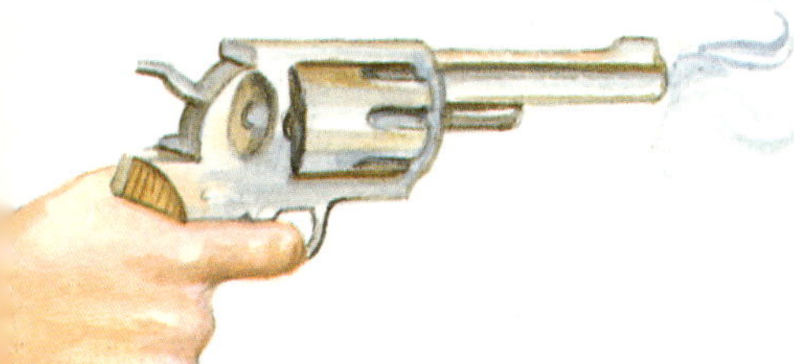

Pistols firing blanks

Artificial blood pellets

Daggers with trick blades

Activity

How to make a prop dagger

You will need a cardboard tube, 70cm long, and 2 sheets of card.

1 Draw and cut out these shapes.

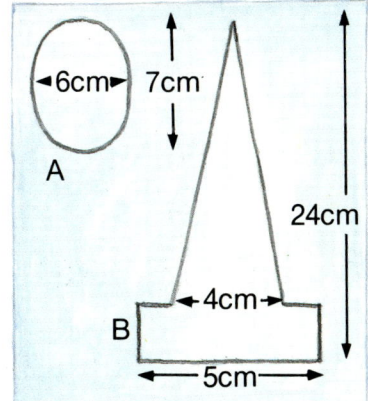

2 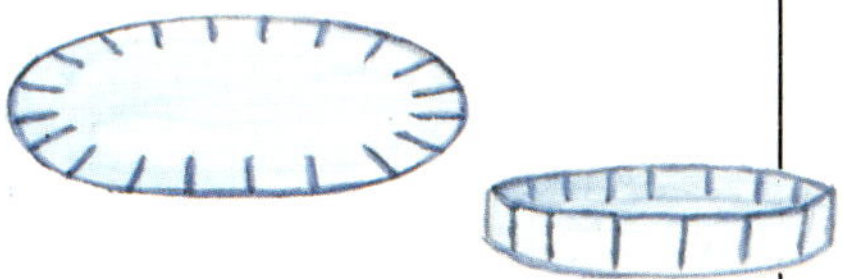 Make a series of 1cm cuts around the edge of piece A and fold up as shown.

3 Stick A to the bottom of the cardboard tube.

4 Push B through C. Then stick C over the top of the cardboard tube.

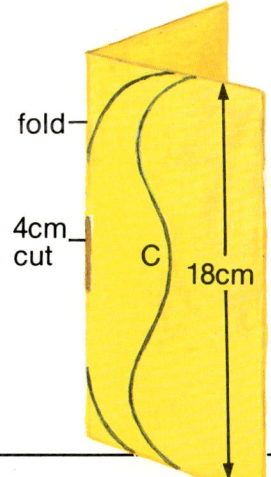

17

Props and Noises Off

In the Chinese Theatre the property man walks among the actors arranging tables, chairs and other props as required. The Japanese property men in the picture above stand behind the dancers as they perform part of a traditional dance.

Music

Musicians are used in every kind of theatre, to help the actors tell the story, or to let the audience know when something important is about to happen.

Indian drummers

Japanese *sumisen*

Trumpeter for fanfares

Elizabethan lutenist and singer

Sound effects

Modern theatres create most of their sound effects on a computer, but it hasn't always been so easy. In Ancient Greece, the sound of thunder was produced by pouring stones from a jar into a brass pot. Thunder can also be made by hanging up a sheet of metal and shaking it fiercely.

Timing for the sound effects and a lighting pattern are worked out at rehearsals then fed into a computer. During the performance a technician operates the computer from a console or control board.

Activity

Make your own sound effects

Horses hooves with yoghurt pots.

Rain, by dropping rice onto an empty tin or drum.

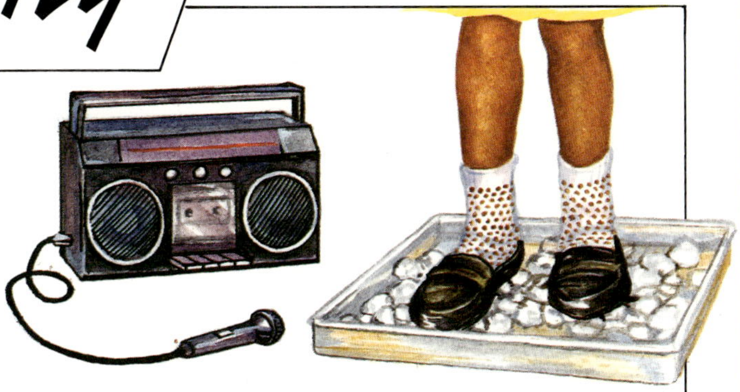

Footsteps, by treading in a gravel box.

Surf, by shaking dried peas inside a shallow cardboard box.

Lighting

A large modern theatre like this can use more than 800 lights to illuminate the stage.

A spotlight can pinpoint a precise area of the stage leaving everywhere else in complete darkness. But to be clearly seen on stage, the actors must be lit from all sides, otherwise there will be shadows all around them.

Try this yourself
Shine a torch directly onto one side of your face and you will see the strange effects created by shadows.

Lighting effects

To suggest the outline of castle battlements, or the shadows cast by leaves, a cut-out stencil called a 'gobo' is placed in front of a light and projected onto a backdrop. To suggest moving clouds, snow or flames, effects projectors are used. You can make one of your own by trying out the activity below.

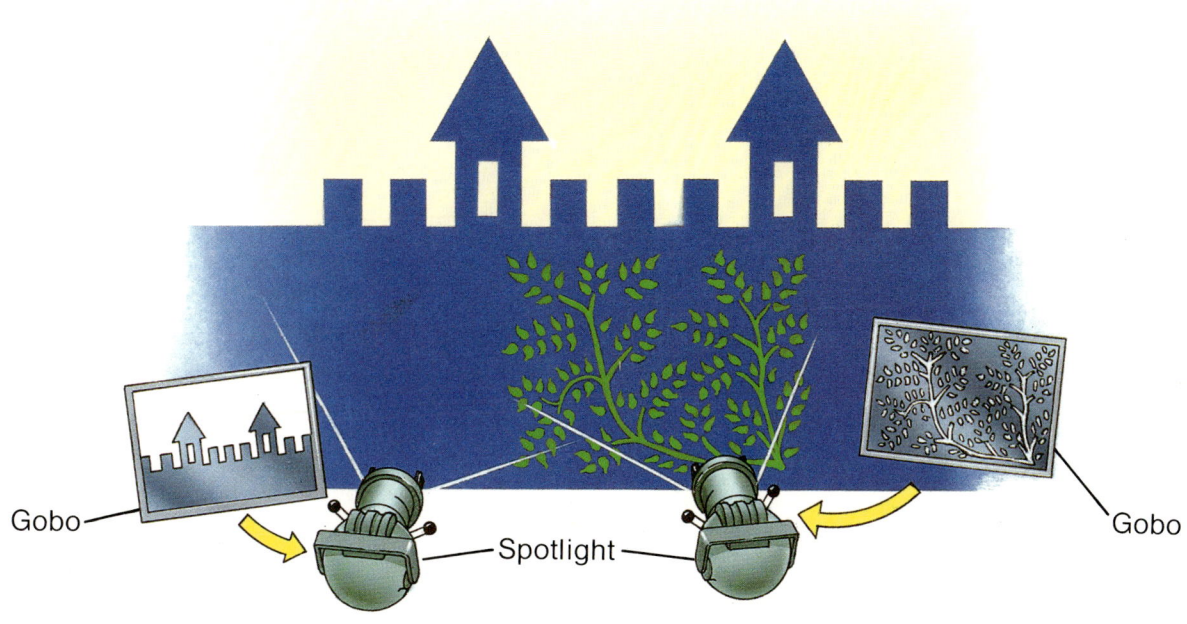

Activity

To make a flame effect

You will need card, red, yellow and orange cellophane, a stick, wire, 2 beads, a light.

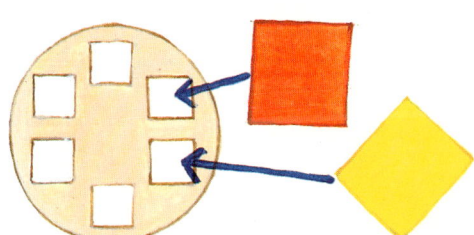

Cut a circle of card and remove several pieces as shown. Stick coloured cellophane over the holes.

Thread the wire through the beads and card and fasten the stick as shown.

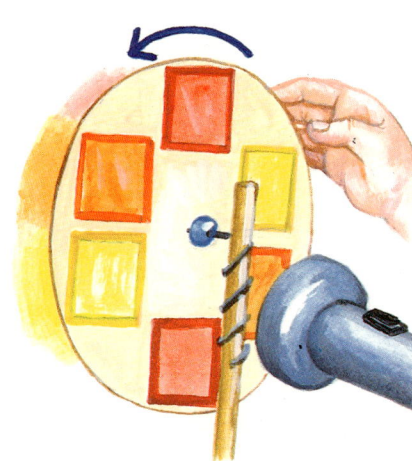

Spin the card, holding the light behind it.

See Inside a Theatre

Can you find?

Actors

Actors have to catch the attention of their audience and hold it throughout the performance. This may sound easy, but actually it takes years of training and practice. Actors must project their voices so that everyone can hear what they are saying or singing, even at the back of the theatre. They must use their faces to show every emotion clearly. Actors used to learn this from books . . . nowadays they watch people in real life and try to copy their expressions on the stage.

Acting technique used to be taught like this.

The actress, Glenda Jackson, in the play *Strange Interlude*.

Every part of the body can be made to show feeling and movement. In India, actors in the Kathakali Theatre learn to describe a bow and arrow using only their hands (*below*). They use their whole bodies to show feelings and emotions (*right*). Indian actors begin each day by exercising eyes, eyebrows and eyelashes.

Kathakali Theatre in Madras, India.

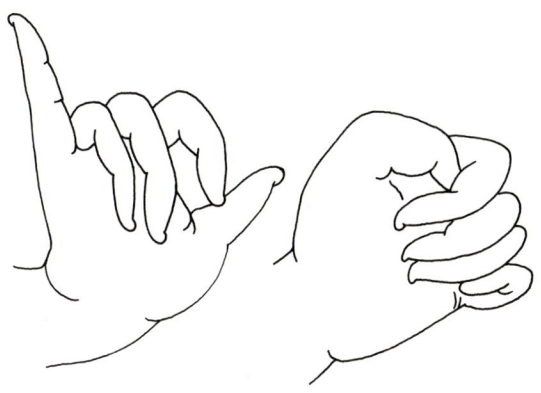

The Russian director, Meyerhold, developed a series of exercises which he called 'biomechanics', to make his actors aware of the whole of their bodies.

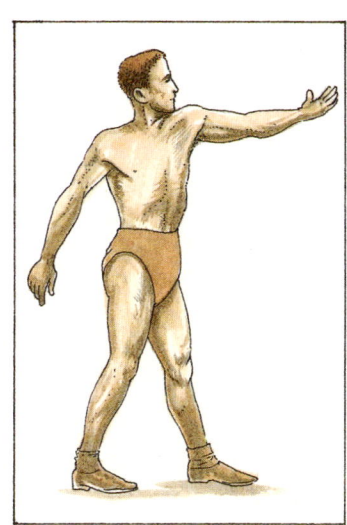

25

With and Without Words

Play scripts

Actors who speak lines use a script. This tells them what to say and where they should be on stage when they say it.

Tybalt Thou, wretched boy, that didst consort him here,
Shalt with him hence.
Romeo This shall determine that.

They fight;

Benvolio Romeo, away, be gone.
The citizens are up, and Tybalt slain.
Stand not amazed. The Prince will doom thee death
If thou art taken. Hence, be gone, away!
Romeo O, I am fortune's fool!
Benvolio Why dost thou stay?

Enter Citizens.

First Citizen Which way ran he that killed Mercutio?
Tybalt, that murderer, which way ran he?
Benvolio There lies that Tybalt.
First Citizen Up, sir, go with me;
I charge thee in the Prince's name, obey.
Enter PRINCE, *attended;* MONTAGUE, CAPULET, *their* Wives, *and* All.

Prince Where are the vile beginners of this fray?
Benvolio O noble Prince, I can discover all
The unlucky manage of this fatal brawl:
There lies the man, slain by young Romeo,
That slew thy kinsman, brave Mercutio.
Lady Capulet Tybalt, my cousin! O my brother's child!
O Prince, O husband! O, the blood is spilled
Of my dear kinsman. Prince as thou art true,
For blood of ours shed blood of Montague.
O cousin, cousin!

The stage directions and the names of characters are written in *italics*.

A scene from *Romeo and Juliet* by William Shakespeare.

Mime

The famous mime artist, Marcel Marceau, performs using only gestures, not words. He tells his story with every movement of his face and body.

Activity

Play this game with your friends.

Make a set of 12 cards and label them like this:

sew on a button
hammer in a nail
clean a window
play a flute
read a book
climb over a wall
roller skate
write a letter
play a game of snooker
clean your teeth
put on a pair of shoes
make a sandwich

Sit in a circle, or around a table. Place the cards face down. Take turns to pick up a card and mime the instruction for your friends to guess. Remember not to use any words! Make up some instructions of your own.

Costumes

Costumes help actors to pretend. They also give the audience clues about what the characters on stage are like. In the Chinese Theatre different colours are used for different types of character: emperors wear yellow, nobles wear red, old people wear brown (*right*).

Activity

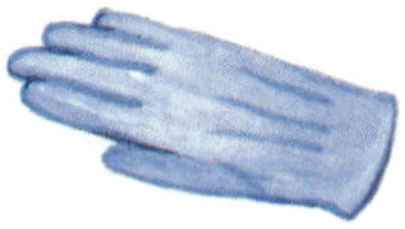

Let's pretend

Collect some old clothes for dressing up. Try some on and see how many different characters you can be.

Here are three ways of dressing Shakespeare's King Richard the Third. Which do you think makes him look most like a king, a soldier, a wicked uncle?

Sir Lawrence Olivier as Richard the Third

Brian Bedford as Richard the Third

Marius Goring as Richard the Third

Characters in costume

witch

devil

snow queen

pied piper

pirate

Masks

Masks are used the world over to hide the actor's face. In Greek tragedies and comedies all the actors wore masks (*top*). In Japanese masked theatre, called 'Noh' theatre, the actors wear wooden masks (*middle*). Noh plays are a mixture of acting, miming and dancing. In India a character from the Ramayana wears a monkey mask (*bottom*).

The fairy queen, Titania, falls in love with the donkey, Bottom, in Shakespeare's *A Midsummer Night's Dream*.

Activity

Make your own animal mask

 Cut out the shape shown.

 Hold it in front of your face and mark the position of your eyes with a pencil. Cut out large eye-holes.

 Cut out a nose shape and fold it as shown.

 Stick the nose tabs through slits in the mask.

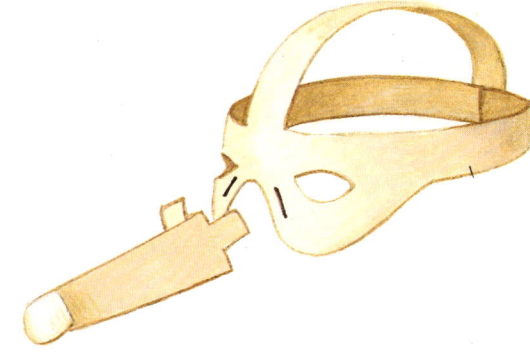

 Cut out ear shapes and stick them to the mask.

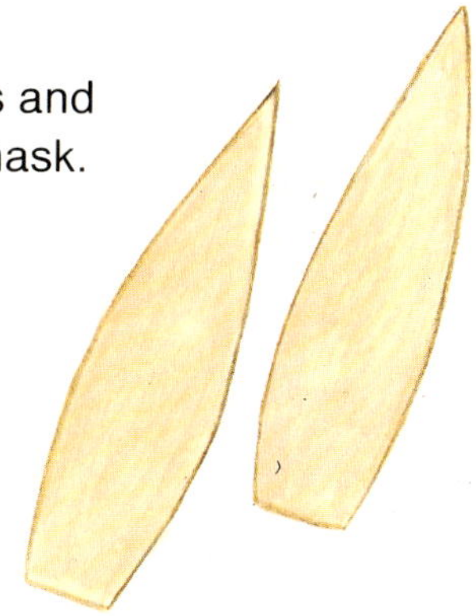

Paint the mask. You can vary the design by changing the shape of the ears and nose, or by adding whiskers and horns!

31

Make-up

Without make-up an actor's face would look blank and lifeless under the glare of the theatre lights. To give expression and character, shadows and highlights are added. Wigs, false eyebrows and beards help to disguise the actor's features.

The make-up of Indian Kathakali actors is applied so thickly that it looks like a mask (*left*). The white paint is mixed with paste, so that when it dries it sticks out from the face.

A Kathakali actor in Madras, India.

Activity

Make yourself up to look old

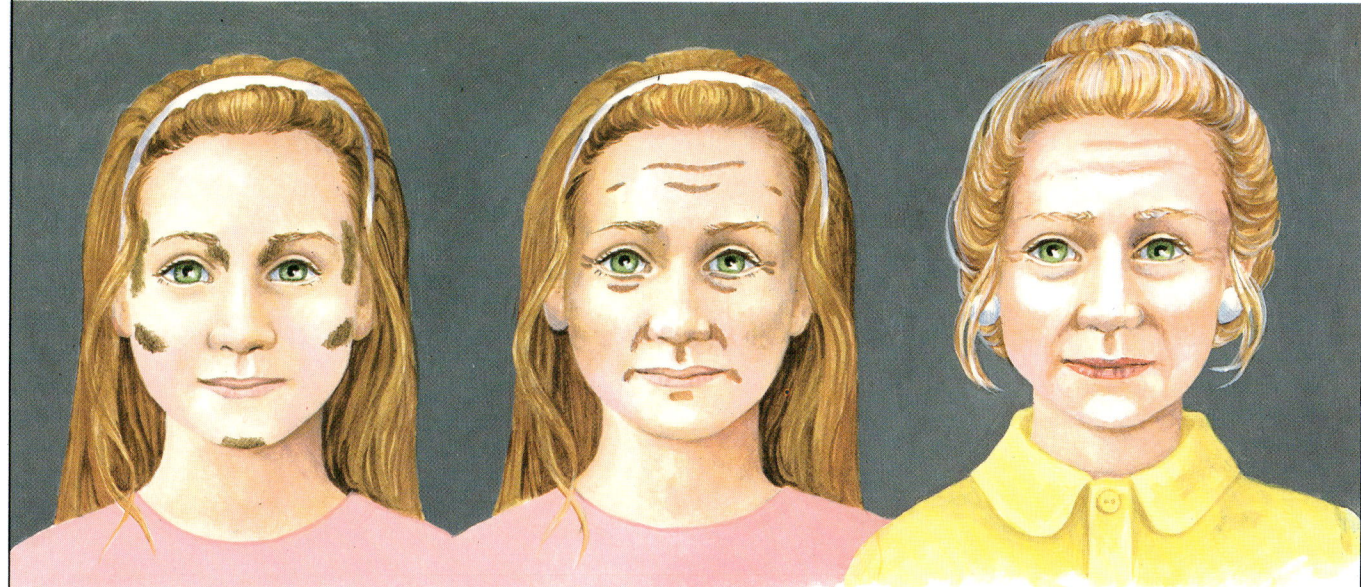

Take a dark make-up stick or face paint and draw dark shadows around your eyes, cheeks and chin.

Add wrinkles to your forehead and at the sides of your eyes, nose and mouth. (Use the lines on your face to guide you.)

With a pale make-up stick draw highlights down the top of your nose and across your cheeks. Now whiten your hair and eyebrows with talcum powder.

See how make-up is applied to make Jos Ackland's face darker and more expressive for his part in the musical *Evita*.

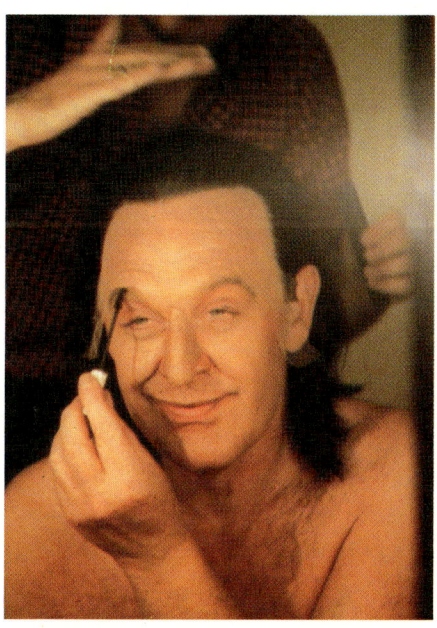

Clowns

Clowns are actors who make people laugh in any way they can.

A Greek clown

Columbine and Harlequin

Activity

Make yourself up as a circus clown

Cover the whole of your face with white face paint.

Paint a large smile onto your lips and cheeks. Paint the tip of your nose red.

Draw a blue line across your upper eyelid, then another from the middle of your eyebrow down your cheek. Now draw on a new pair of eyebrows.

Grimaldi and his frog

Japanese clowns

The clown Pulcinella has become a popular puppet character in many parts of Europe. In England he is called Punch, in France Polchinelle and in Russia Petrushka.

Coco the Clown

Puppet Theatre

The actors in this play are puppets. Every movement is controlled by the children-puppeteers working above the curtain.

A detail from a Chinese handscroll, the *Hundred Children*.

Puppets the world over come in all sizes.

Chinese glove puppets are not much bigger than a human hand . . .

. . . but these puppets from Indonesia, telling a traditional story, are life-sized.

Glove puppets are the simplest to use and make. Perhaps you could make one yourself.

A rod puppet can be made using just a wooden spoon.

As you can see, string puppets (sometimes called marionettes) can be quite difficult to operate.

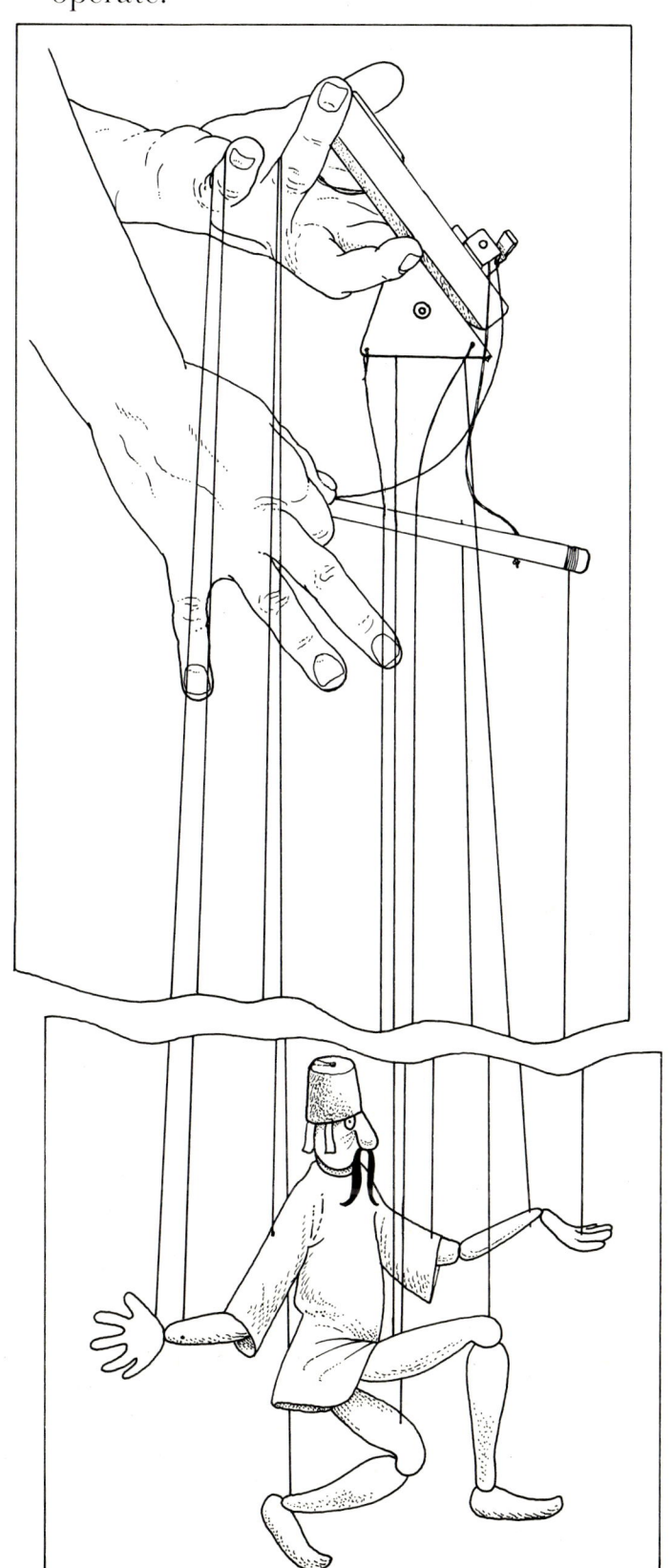

Bunraku

Bunraku is the name for Japanese puppet theatre. Each puppet is made with great care by a skilled craftsworker. Nearly every part can be moved separately by the puppeteer: for example, the eyebrows lift up and down, the mouth opens and closes and the eyes swivel.

This picture shows the wires and levers needed to work the hand.

The puppeteers of the Bunraku Theatre are seen on stage with their puppets, dressed in black so as not to distract the audience. Three puppeteers work the puppet; one for the body and right arm, one for the left arm and one for the feet. The audience listens as the story of the play is told by a narrator. A musician accompanies him on the *sumisen*.

Shadow puppets

Shadow puppets entertain people in many parts of the world . . .

China

Indonesia

Greece

Activity

Make your own shadow puppet theatre

Cut the characters in your story from card. Use paper clips to make the moving parts.

Stick rods to the back of each character.

Make the screen by stretching a piece of white cotton material over a wooden frame such as the back of a chair. Shine a light onto the back of the screen and move your puppet backwards and forwards across the surface.

39

Travelling Theatre

Roll up! Roll up! The theatre is coming to town.

There have always been troupes of strolling players touring the countryside and giving performances in the open air. More than three hundred years ago, the great French playwright, Molière, began his career in a troupe like this one.

This modern theatre company travels by lorry, setting up its tent in parks, or wherever it will fit! Like Molière's troupe, the actors use song and dance as well as story-telling to entertain their audience.

The London Bubble travelling theatre tent.

In the USSR, after the Revolution, trains were used to bring theatre to the countryside. Through plays, actors told people about the new ideas.

Theatre is sometimes used in the same way today. These Indian actors are showing their audience ways to keep healthy.

Activity

Stage your own play

The story: either you can make up your own, or borrow someone else's (a fairy tale for example).

The stage: where are you going to perform your play, inside or outside? Where will the audience sit?

Costumes: make your own costumes using old clothes or bits of material.

Props and scenery: many plays today use little or no scenery. For props everyday things around the house will do, or you can cut out and paint your own.

Rehearsals: rehearse each scene carefully, making sure everybody knows what they are supposed to be doing. Have at least one dress rehearsal with costumes and props.

Publicity: design a poster and a programme to tell the audience about the play.

The opening night: everyone is nervous. It is time to put on make-up and costumes. On you go and good luck!

Index

Ackland, Jos 33
activities: dagger 17; dressing up 28; effects 19, 21; make-up 34; masks 31; mime 27; puppets 37, 39; put on a play 42–3; toy theatre 12
actors 24–5

backstage 15
Bedford, Brian 29
Behan, Brendan 14
Bunraku theatre 38

China 18, 28, 36, 39
clowns 34–5
Coco the Clown 35
Columbine and Harlequin 34
Corneille, Pierre 14
costumes 15, 28–9, 42

director, work of a 13

Elizabethan theatre 11, 18

Globe theatre 11
glove puppets 36, 37

Goring, Marius 29
Greece 10, 19, 30, 39
Grimaldi, Joseph 35

India 18, 25, 30, 32, 41
Indonesia 36, 39

Jackson, Glenda 24,
Japan 10, 18, 30, 35

Kabuki theatre 10
Kathakali theatre 25, 32
Kenny, Sean 14

lighting 20–1
London Bubble Theatre 8, 40

machinery, stage 16
make-up 32–3
Marceau, Marcel 27
masks 30–1
medieval plays 10
Meyerhold V. E. 25
mime 27
Molière, Jean Baptiste 40
musicians 18, 38

Noh plays 30

Olivier, Sir Lawrence 29

props 17, 18, 42
Pulcinella 35
puppets 36–9

Ramayana 30
revolving stages 16

scripts 26
sets, stage 14, 15
shadow puppets 39
Shakespeare, William 11, 26, 29, 30
sound effects 19
stories 8–9
sumisen (Japan) 18, 38

Torelli, Giacomo 14
travelling theatres 40–1

USSR 41

weapons 17

Acknowledgements

The publishers would like to thank the following for kindly supplying photographs for this book:

Page 8 London Bubble; 10 ZEFA (top), The Mansell Collection (bottom); 11 The Mansell Collection (top), The Royal Exchange Theatre Company, Manchester (bottom); 14 Osterreichische Nationalbibliothek (top), Donald Cooper Photostage (left), Victoria & Albert Museum (right); 18 The Hutchison Library; 19 Zoe Dominic Photography; 20 Zoe Dominic Photography; 24 The Mansell Collection (left), Donald Cooper Photostage (right); 25 ZEFA; 26 Donald Cooper Photostage; 27 J. A. Hamilton Photography; 28 Spectrum Colour Library; 29 John Vickers (left), Zoe Dominic Photography (middle), Angus McBean (right); 30 Zoe Dominic Photography (left), Ancient Art & Architecture Collection (right); 32 ZEFA; 33 Zoe Dominic Photography; 34 Ancient Art & Architecture Collection (left), Michael Holford (right); 35 The Bridgeman Art Library (top), The Hulton-Deutsch Collection (bottom); 36 Michael Holford (top), Xinhua News Agency (left), Werner Forman Archive (right); 38 The Hutchison Library; 40 London Bubble; 41 David King Collection.

Front cover The Bridgeman Art Library (left), ZEFA (right); Back cover The Royal Exchange Theatre Company, Manchester.

Picture Research: Elaine Willis